MOTIVATING
PEOPLE

Iain Maitland

Iain Maitland is an author and lecturer specialising in key management issues. He has written more than 20 books, including *Getting a Result* and *Motivating People* for the Institute of Personnel and Development. He is also the author of another title in the IPD's Training Extras series, *Managing Your Time*.

TRAINING EXTRAS is a comprehensive series covering all the crucial management skill areas. Each booklet includes the key issues, helpful starting points and practical advice in a concise and lively style. Together, they form an accessible library reflecting current best practice – ideal for study or quick reference.

Other titles in the series include:

Asking Questions Ian MacKay

Businesslike Budgeting Eric Parsloe and Raymond Wright

Customer Care Roland and Frances Bee

Listening Skills Ian MacKay

The Manager as Coach and Mentor Eric Parsloe

Managing Your Time Iain Maitland

Negotiating, Persuading and Influencing Alan Fowler

The Selection Interview Penny Hackett

Working in Teams Alison Hardingham

MOTIVATING
PEOPLE

Iain Maitland

INSTITUTE OF PERSONNEL AND DEVELOPMENT

Design and typesetting by Paperweight
Printed in Great Britain by
Short Run Press, Exeter

British Library Cataloguing in Publication Data
A catalogue record for this book is available from the
British Library

ISBN
0-85292-585-9 (pack of five)

INSTITUTE OF PERSONNEL
AND DEVELOPMENT

IPD House, Camp Road, London SW19 4UX
Tel.: 0181 971 9000   Fax: 0181 263 3333
Registered office as above. Registered Charity No. 1038333
A company limited by guarantee. Registered in England No. 2931892

Contents

1

 **Introducing Motivation**

So what is 'motivation'? It can be defined quite simply as 'the force or process which causes individuals to act in a specific way'. Of course, there is more to it than is implied by this short definition. It is a good idea to start finding out about motivation by looking briefly at the theory of motivating people before going on to think about how this can be applied in practice, in your specific workplace.

Motivating people: the theory

Numerous theories have been put forward about motivation and what it is, and three in particular have retained their credibility over a period of time *and* provide a concise but comprehensive introduction to the subject:

- Maslow's 'Hierarchy of Needs'
- Herzberg's 'Two-Factor Theory'
- Vroom's 'Expectancy Theory'

Maslow's Hierarchy of Needs

Probably the best-known of the motivational theorists, Abraham Maslow was an American psychologist who believed that all individuals have a set hierarchy of needs which they want to be satisfied. This 'Hierarchy of Needs' is shown in Figure 1.1. According to Maslow, an individual's first need is to obtain sufficient air, food and water to survive (physiological need). Once he or she has achieved this, then *more* air, food and water will not motivate – safety needs will instead. As soon as someone is free from danger and attack, then he or she will be motivated by social needs – friendships, and the like.

An individual moves up through the need for self-esteem and recognition from others until his or her self-actualisation needs are satisfied, and he or she feels completely developed and fulfilled, having achieved as much as possible. However, if lower-level needs suddenly stop being met at any time, then the individual will be motivated again by those ones. For example,

Figure 1.1

MASLOW'S HIERARCHY OF NEEDS

a man is chatting to a friend on a street corner, thus satisfying his social needs. If a lunatic brandishing a knife comes around the corner, then the man's safety needs are no longer being met, because he is not free from danger or attack. Accordingly, he runs away – more concerned about satisfying those lower, safety needs than the higher, social ones!

Attempts have been made to relate Maslow's theory to employees' requirements in the workplace. Physiological needs are here concerned with pay and other, similar benefits. Safety needs are linked to such matters as job security, sick pay and pension schemes, sufficient rest periods, protection from unfair actions and physical safety. Social needs are associated with a sense of belonging, friendly and helpful colleagues and superiors. Self-esteem needs may be met by recognition and praise from supervisors and managers, plus the prospects of transfers and promotions. Self-actualisation needs can be satisfied by providing fulfilling, interesting jobs, where abilities are used extensively.

Herzberg's Two-Factor Theory

Frederick Herzberg suggested that there are two equally important groups of factors relevant to motivating staff – as listed in Figure 1.2. He argued that hygiene factors (or 'dissatisfiers') do not actually motivate, but need to be at least satisfactory if they are not to demotivate people. As an example, a safe and healthy workplace will not in itself encourage employees to work

Figure 1.2

HERZBERG'S TWO-FACTOR THEORY

HYGIENE FACTORS	MOTIVATORS
Working conditions	Work itself
Pay	Responsibility
Job security	Sense of achievement
Work relationships	Recognition
Supervisory and management practices	Prospects for advancement
Company policies and administration	

harder and/or better but satisfies them enough so that other factors can motivate them. Nonetheless, if working conditions are unpleasant, then people will feel demotivated, and these other elements will simply not work.

If hygiene factors are all in place and satisfactory, Herzberg claimed that five key factors are then able to motivate staff: challenging and interesting work; responsibility for tasks and duties carried out; a sense of having achieved something worthwhile; recognition of completed work, effort and performance; and the possibility of personal development, transfer and promotion. Clearly, Herzberg believed that the job itself is the main motivator in the work environment, and that all the other possible influences are of no more than secondary importance.

Vroom's Expectancy Theory

Developing from the 'Hierarchy of Needs' and 'Two-Factor' theories, V.H. Vroom put forward his 'Expectancy Theory', as illustrated in Figure 1.3. He believed that there are two component parts of motivation: an individual's wants *and* his or her expectation of achieving them. He used the word 'valency' to describe the level of a particular want, with a high valency indicating a strong desire for the want, and a low valency suggesting that it is less important to the person and thus less likely to motivate.

Nevertheless, if a high valency is to act as a motivator, the individual also needs to feel that the specific want can be satisfied. For example, an employee may have a strong desire to obtain a particular type of company

Figure 1.3

VROOM'S EXPECTANCY THEORY

VALENCY × EXPECTANCY

⇓

MOTIVATION

⇓

ACTION

⇓

RESULTS

⇓

SATISFACTION

car, such as a BMW instead of a Cavalier. If he or she knows this is achievable because BMWs are provided for the top salespeople, then he or she will attempt to take whatever action is needed to produce the required result, and satisfy that want. If it does not appear to be achievable, then there is little point in working harder and/or better. He or she is not motivated.

Motivating people: in practice

Clearly, all of these theories are valid, although they each have their own approach and emphasise some factors more or less than others. Nevertheless, you have the responsibility of translating such theory into practice, and actually motivating those around you in the work environment. Thus, you need to contemplate the practicalities of:

- being a good leader
- working as a team
- improving jobs
- developing people
- paying staff
- providing a safe and healthy workplace.

Being a good leader

People and the relationships between them are probably the biggest influence upon motivation, for better or worse. You can almost certainly have a huge and positive impact here, simply by being a good leader. If not one already, you can improve by understanding your personal, departmental and organisational goals, leading by example and then motivating others to follow your lead by involving them in everything you do.

Working as a team

Likewise, teamwork has an absolutely vital role to play in motivating people. As the leader of what you hope will prove to be a successful team, you must be able to identify the characteristics of a winning team so that you all have something to aim for. You should also recognise team members as individuals with differing wants and needs – and treat them as such! Drawing on this knowledge, you will need to employ various teambuilding tactics in order to create and subsequently maintain a cohesive and effective team.

Improving jobs

If employees are affected by the people who work alongside them, then they will obviously be influenced as much by the jobs that they are doing for the firm. Again, you may be in a position to exert a positive influence in this area. Accordingly, you need to appreciate the importance of job enjoyment to people, and be capable of appraising employees and their employment to see how well suited they are. If they are ill matched – and feel dissatisfied and demotivated as a result – you will wish to re-arrange their workload to improve matters.

Developing people

Everyone wants to feel fulfilled at work, that they are making the most of their talents and abilities and are progressing as far as they can. To achieve this, you must encourage self-development amongst your team, helping them to set their own standards and targets to work within and towards. Staff need to be trained as well, to give them the skills and knowledge necessary to do their present *and* future jobs properly. You should assess employees regularly too, so you can see how they are developing and if – or hopefully when – they are ready to be transferred and promoted to more demanding, higher-status jobs.

Paying staff

Pay and other financial benefits can inspire people to work harder and better – or demotivate them if these are seen as unacceptable. Although you may not have much influence here, you should consider pay levels within your business to judge if they are satisfactory; think about the different pay systems which operate and their respective pros and cons; and contemplate the overall pay package being provided, taking account of such benefits as sick pay, health insurance and pension schemes.

Providing a safe and healthy workplace

Similarly, the work environment can either make people feel good or demotivate them if it is not at least satisfactory so far as they are concerned. Hopefully, you will be in a position to ensure safe working conditions and build up a healthy environment. At the same time, you may find it useful to know something about the law in this field, to make certain that your firm is meeting its legal obligations to its employees.

Further reading

HAGEMANN G. *The Motivation Manual*. Aldershot, Gower, 1992.

MAITLAND I. *Getting a Result*. London, Institute of Personnel and Development, 1994.

ROBERTSON I., SMITH M. and COOPER D. *Motivation: Strategies, theory and practice*. (2nd edn) London, Institute of Personnel Management, 1992.

SARGENT A. *Turning People On*. London, Institute of Personnel Management, 1990.

2

Being a Good Leader

Many of the key ingredients of motivation can be influenced or improved by you, to make people increase the quantity and quality of their work. Being a good leader is important, and you can go some way towards becoming one if you understand your goals, lead by example and motivate others to follow you.

Understanding your goals

A 'good leader' could be said to be 'someone who motivates and co-ordinates his or her team so that their individual and group skills, knowledge and experiences are used effectively, and goals are achieved'. You cannot begin to set about motivating and co-ordinating people until you – and they – know exactly what they are aiming to achieve. Therefore you need to:

- pinpoint your goals
- check their suitability
- notify your team.

Pinpoint your goals

You have to be able to identify each and every goal that you and your colleagues are working towards – personal, departmental and organisational ones, *and* those in the short, medium and long terms. It is not enough simply to have a rough idea or a gut feeling: these are just too vague and abstract, and are unlikely to win the support and commitment of your team. You need to know *precisely* where you are going, how to get there and when you want to arrive. It is also imperative that all of these various goals are consistent and complement one another – in short, that they are all moving in the same direction.

Check their suitability

Logically, you will be setting personal goals for individuals and teams to achieve, which will in turn combine to help the department and/or firm to reach overall goals. In order to motivate staff to work towards them, these goals need to be *challenging* – demanding enough to stretch people, so that the fullest possible use of abilities has to be made. They also have to be specific, so that progress can be measured and checked, and amendments made, when necessary. Equally significant, they must be *achievable* – but only just, and through maximum work-rate and performance – because failure is demoralising and can have an adverse affect on an individual, and his or her immediate colleagues.

Notify your team

Conscious of your goals and which ones are going to be allocated to certain individuals, you should then make sure that they are clearly stated and well understood by everyone involved. Each person and team should have agreed targets to pursue – to produce or sell so many units, or whatever. Similarly, they must be given particular standards which need to be adhered to – health and safety laws must be kept, tasks have to be completed within a set timescale, and so on. It is sensible to explain the reason for any instructions and try to reach agreement at all times: an informed and involved workforce will always work harder and better than they would otherwise do.

Leading by example

Probably one of the best ways of motivating people to work towards personal, departmental and organisational goals is to lead by example. This is a key skill which can be developed successfully by contemplating and subsequently blending together a mix of three factors:

- leadership qualities
- leadership styles
- varying situations

Leadership qualities

All successful leaders have certain personal attributes in common. They are self-disciplined in everything they do: attendance, time-keeping, appearance, work practices and so on. If you take time off with a cold, are late, look scruffy, do not use safety equipment properly or whatever, then your bad attitude and habits will affect those around you who will soon become equally sloppy and also demotivated. By contrast, good leaders show commitment, striving constantly to improve their work-rate and performance. If you are laid back about your work, then your colleagues will be as well. You may feel you have the right to take it easy from time to time – unfortunately, they will often think the same applies to them.

Fairness is a key characteristic which all leaders need to possess in abundance *and* at all times. You have to be seen to be fair in everything you do, praising when and where due, disciplining and correcting where appropriate, and encouraging and congratulating those who deserve it. Moral courage is important, too: you need to be brave enough to tackle difficult problems – to admit you have made a mistake or an error of judgement, or to discipline a slack or disruptive employee. Likewise, you have to be able to make critical decisions – to dismiss a person if necessary, or to lay off surplus part-timers.

Winning leaders should balance their potentially more forceful qualities, such as self-discipline and moral courage, by having a caring attitude. You should show interest in your staff as individuals, by knowing their names and something about them, *and* understanding the good and bad aspects of their work, empathising with their difficulties etc. The best leaders are, also, loyal to their team. You need to demonstrate trust, typically by letting people get on with their tasks without interference. Credit them with their successes rather than claiming these as your own. Similarly, do not blame them for your failings. Support colleagues in public, rather than criticising them behind their backs. On page 10 is a questionnaire that may help you to decide whether you are a good leader or not.

Leadership styles

These are various styles that can be adopted by a successful leader, ranging from the autocratic to the democratic, as highlighted in Figure 2.1 At the autocratic extreme, the leader identifies a problem, considers possible solutions and makes a decision, subsequently telling his or her team what to do. They have no say in the matter at all. Alternatively, the leader can reach the decision and then try to 'sell' it to the team, typically by stressing any benefits related to it. He or she recognises that there may have been some adverse reaction to the most autocratic approach. Nevertheless, the decision has been made and will remain the same, come what may.

Becoming more democratic, the leader may present a problem to the team, putting forward the potential solutions and a tentative decision and asking for their responses, and own contributions, as appropriate. He or she makes the final decision though, but is open and receptive to the comments and suggestions of others. At a much more democratic level, the leader states the problem, identifies the prospective solutions with his or her team and then everyone reaches a decision together, by joint

QUESTIONNAIRE: ARE YOU A GOOD LEADER?

Saying 'yes' to all these questions suggests you are a good leader. If not, you need to improve!

	Yes	Sometimes	No
Do you know exactly what you and your team are supposed to be doing?	❏	❏	❏
Do you set demanding but achievable goals for team members?	❏	❏	❏
Can these goals be monitored and measured easily?	❏	❏	❏
Do team members know precisely what they should be doing?	❏	❏	❏
Are you conscientious?	❏	❏	❏
Are you hardworking?	❏	❏	❏
Do you set a good example?	❏	❏	❏
Are you a fair and reasonable leader?	❏	❏	❏
Are you willing to take tough decisions?	❏	❏	❏
Are you genuinely interested in your team members?	❏	❏	❏
Do you trust them?	❏	❏	❏
Do you support them?	❏	❏	❏
Do you adjust your leadership style according to circumstances?	❏	❏	❏
Do you treat team members as equals?	❏	❏	❏
Do you involve them at all times?	❏	❏	❏
Do you encourage and acknowledge their progress and successes?	❏	❏	❏
Do you adjust their goals as and when necessary?	❏	❏	❏

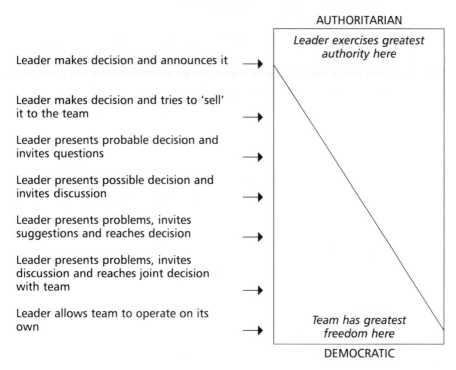

Figure 2.1

TYPES OF LEADERSHIP STYLE

agreement. Assuming that this fits into overall, organisational policy, it will be adhered to by everyone.

Varying situations

Not surprisingly, the style you should choose – and it will inevitably change regularly – will vary according to the particular circumstances which exist at any given time. There are three major influences: you, the work involved, and the team you are responsible for leading. You may have strong feelings about a certain style, believing (as many do) that a democratic approach usually motivates people more than an autocratic one. Your own position in relation to those around you is significant: if you are relatively new and uncertain of your place, you might be fairly autocratic to start with, but gradually less so as you become established, popular and trusted – *and* more trusting of your team too. At times you may nonetheless have firm opinions, and want them to prevail, whatever anyone thinks.

The nature and complexity of the work is of some relevance. Perhaps it is ambiguous or beyond the (decision-making) skills, knowledge and expertise of the team, so you need to take charge. Alternatively, it may well be within their capabilities – indeed, they might know more about it than you! – so they should have some input. Time may be of the essence on occasions: a quick decision has to be made, perhaps because it is an emergency. There is no time for any discussion: 'Do it, and do it now!' has to be the immediate response in this situation.

Evidently, the team is a huge influence on your leadership style. In particular, members may have specific views about how they wish to be led. Some people want to be told what to do, whereas others prefer a degree of choice and freedom. Staff may wish to become more involved in issues that interest them, and less in those that do not. Their levels of skill, knowledge and experience in given areas are significant as well: if they know more about something, it is sensible to draw on that by adopting a more democratic style, and vice versa if they know relatively little.

Motivating others

Hopefully, if you understand your goals and lead by example, you will persuade people to follow your lead and work towards achieving the goals set at personal, departmental and organisational levels. Nonetheless, there is more you can do yourself to motivate those around you. The following are the key interpersonal skills that usually need to be employed regularly on a face-to-face basis:

- discussing and agreeing
- encouraging and acknowledging
- reviewing and amending

Discussing and agreeing

Goals, targets and standards should be set, whenever possible, after talking about them with staff. People need to be given the chance to discuss overall goals (at whatever level), make comments and suggestions for amending and/or improving their workload, and so on. They deserve to be treated as equals with respect being shown for what they feel, think and have to say. This all helps to make them more involved and part of what is happening. Inevitably, employees will always work harder and better towards *agreed* goals, targets and standards than ones that have simply been imposed upon them without any form of consultation – even though, in reality, they may be one and the same!

Encouraging and acknowledging

It is just as important that employees are watched – albeit discreetly at times – and encouraged to progress towards reaching and maintaining standards and achieving targets. Their progress should be acknowledged often, and any successes must be congratulated warmly. Sincere praise and signs of appreciation – even something as simple as a smile and a thumbs-up sign – give people a sense of achievement, and make them feel they are making a worthwhile contribution. Be supportive if they fail, telling them why and where they went wrong, and showing them how to improve, without blaming or embarrassing them. Recognising their strengths and making fair and constructive criticisms about their weaknesses leaves people wanting to do better next time around.

Reviewing and amending

Working with your team, you should continually evaluate and review goals, targets and standards in the light of team members' subsequent workrate and performance. Ensure that staff have the opportunity to put across their views and wishes – again, this means treating them as respected equals. Where relevant, it is best to make amendments to bring certain goals, targets and standards within reach of people's capabilities. Constant failure to achieve overambitious goals will distress and demotivate, affecting not only the person concerned but also those working alongside him or her, who have to deal with anger and resentment, and take on additional, excess work.

Further reading

ADAIR J. *The Skills of Leadership*. Aldershot, Gower, 1984.

HONEY P. *Face to Face Skills*. Aldershot, Gower, 1988.

THORNELY N. and LEES D. *Leadership: The art of motivation*. London, Random House, 1994.

3

Working as a Team

In addition to good leadership, teamwork has a major role to play in motivation. If you are to lead a winning team, you need to be able to identify its particular characteristics, recognise its members as individuals in their own right as well as part of the team, and then employ various teambuilding tactics so that everyone works together, and successfully.

Identifying team characteristics

A 'winning team' might be described as a 'group of individuals working with one another to achieve common goals'. In order to develop and motivate the people you are in charge of, you have to be aware of the main features of a successful team. This gives you and your colleagues a framework to work within. Such a team is usually:

- unified
- self-organised
- self-supporting
- small.

Unified

All the members of a winning team are unified, with everyone pulling together in the same direction to complete a specific job and/or reach a shared goal, typically to increase output or sales by a certain amount over a given period of time. Generally, the job and/or goal can best be achieved by working collectively rather than individually. An effective team has its own unique identity, with members feeling a sense of belonging to it: production-line workers know 'their' team is responsible for producing goods, salespeople for selling them, and so forth.

Self-organised

Successful teams tend to create their own structure, with members often adopting different roles at key times, according to needs and abilities. Someone with experience of a particular task may organise the others for a while, with another member taking charge for a subsequent activity with which he or she is the most familiar. An informal and unspoken code of behaviour will develop alongside this structure, and all members will abide by it. Unwritten rules might include going outside the workroom to smoke a cigarette, notifying colleagues on completion of a certain task, or checking with another member before carrying out a specific duty.

Self-supporting

Members of a winning team inevitably co-operate fully with one another to do a job and/or fulfil a goal, sharing out tasks according to ability, advising and guiding when needed, co-ordinating duties and tackling problems together. They all support one another, typically by workmates taking on certain tasks if one person is overworked or experiencing difficulties in some way. They inevitably cover one another as well, eg clocking the latecomer in or the early leaver out. A very strong sense of unity and belonging is especially noticeable at these times.

Small

By and large, successful teams are relatively small so that members can organise and manage themselves: dividing up tasks fairly, sharing ideas and opinions openly, identifying problems swiftly, and remedying them promptly. Five has often been suggested as the ideal number – more than that and discussions will take longer, with one or two team members dominating whilst others do not contribute fully. Cliques may form, too. Fewer than five, and there may be insufficient skills, knowledge and expertise available to do the job properly. Whatever the precise number – and you may not be in a position to choose – an odd number is more sensible as this avoids a 50:50 split when decisions have to be made.

Recognising team members

It is important that you do not view the members of your team in the same way – effectively, as some form of 'identikit' person. They are all individuals with different personalities, likes and dislikes, and ever-changing wants and needs, and should be seen as such. Nevertheless, some may have similar features to the 'typical' team members listed below – but be careful not to attribute a complete set of characteristics to a colleague just because he or she appears to have one or two in common. Get to know each person individually! 'Typical' team members include the:

- thinker
- organiser
- doer
- teamworker
- checker
- evaluator.

The thinker

This member could also be called the 'ideas person'. He or she is concerned with the overview of what is going to be done, and often has lots of (rather hit-and-miss) ideas and suggestions. The thinker may not be so good with the details, though! He or she could be artistic and creative, and perhaps tense and nervous on occasions, too. Invariably, this team member needs to be handled carefully, with praise, encouragement and even flattery now and then, if he or she is not to become sulky and withdrawn.

The organiser

Working alongside the more creative thinker may be the organiser, who usually attends to the practical details, arranging and allocating tasks and duties, drawing up schedules, rotas and the like. He or she tends to be calm, disciplined, methodical and efficient if – and often *only* if – everything is well planned and structured. The organiser can sometimes be accused of having a head-down, blinkered approach, and of being dogmatic and inflexible. He or she may find it hard to work effectively in vague and/or changing circumstances. You should be able to deal with him or her easily, *if* you can provide plenty of charts and timetables!

The doer

This member makes things happen, and has a real 'get up and go' attitude! He or she is an action person – extrovert, impulsive, impatient of indecision and waffle. The doer often dominates a team, leading first and thinking second. He or she may be rather temperamental and argumentative, and can become frustrated if everything does not work out as expected. You could find it difficult to restrain him or her from pressing ahead regardless; you need to exert a calming, rational influence in order to channel those formidable energies along the right lines.

The teamworker

Not surprisingly, the teamworker is keen to unify the team, and acts in a supporting and cohesive manner towards his or her colleagues, trying to develop and carry out their ideas rather than his or her own. He or she is caring and likeable, loyal and friendly – a 'people person'! The teamworker dislikes confrontation and arguments, and may be rather indecisive on occasion, not wanting to offend anyone. He or she is sometimes not very noticeable, tending to fade into the background. You will probably have to encourage and persuade him or her to come forward with comments and suggestions and to be more positive.

The checker

As the name implies, the checker – or double-checker! – likes to keep a close watch on how everything is progressing. He or she may describe his or her key features as being conscientious and meticulous. Others might say he or she is compulsive and obsessive! Whatever the description, the checker does play an essential role, continually reminding the team of the need for urgency (if appropriate), helping it to progress on schedule and to complete work on time. You may find yourself having to soothe the checker's worries now and then, and to mediate between him or her and the other team members when friction arises, as it will inevitably do from time to time.

The evaluator

This member provides a good balance against the more instinctive thinker and doer. He or she is often slightly detached from the team, may be rather aloof and distant, and tends to analyse all ideas, suggestions and actions carefully and objectively before reaching an opinion. Although the evaluator may not be especially liked, his or her views are usually listened to with respect, and are accepted by the other team members. He or she performs the useful functions of slowing down impulsive colleagues and vetoing any 'extreme' plans of theirs. You might wish to draw him or her into the team more during discussions.

Employing teambuilding tactics

Ideally, you and your colleagues will already be showing signs of becoming a winning team, with you as its leader. There are several steps you can take personally to complete the process, including these in particular:

- establish a compact team
- agree a common aim

- know the individual members
- maintain good communications.

Establish a compact team

Obviously, you can help to encourage a successful team to develop by restricting membership where possible – perhaps to five, which is probably the best number in most circumstances. Thought also needs to be given where appropriate to those people who are to comprise the team. It may be unwise to have two employees who are going to be 'thinkers', constantly clashing over their original and distinctive views. Likewise, it would be inadvisable to have too many 'doers', each trying to dominate and go in different directions and *now*! Attempt to bring together the right mix – thinker, organiser, doer and so on – who will support and check one another as you would wish them to do.

Agree a common aim

Ensure that everyone knows what their workload involves, what the standards and targets are and where they are supposed to be going in terms of personal, departmental and organisational goals. Try to group together associated tasks and duties, giving these to the same team, because this will consequently encourage the members to organise the work amongst themselves and to co-operate with one another in order to complete it successfully, and on time. Make certain that the whole team agrees about what they are doing, when *and* why, because this will help them to get together and work as a cohesive unit.

Know the individual members

Quite clearly, you need to get to know each member of the team as well as possible, in order to identify their own specific blend of features, likes and dislikes, strengths and weaknesses. You will need to deal with each person in a different manner. For example, the doer may have to be encouraged to slow down, wait, think and listen to what others say *before* having a go at the work. The teamworker may need to be persuaded to present his or her views to the team. On occasion you may have to mediate between members, for example between the doer and the checker, getting them to sit down, listen to each other and respect their different views.

Maintain good communications

Communication – between you and the team and amongst team members

QUESTIONNAIRE: ARE YOU COMMUNICATING WELL?

If you and your team can say 'always' to these questions, then you are communicating successfully. If not, there is room for improvement!

	Always	Sometimes	Never
Are you well prepared when you communicate?	❏	❏	❏
Before communicating, do you know why you are going to communicate?	❏	❏	❏
Do you calculate what you want to put across and achieve?	❏	❏	❏
Do you establish your facts and check them?	❏	❏	❏
Do you consider the different aspects and alternatives involved?	❏	❏	❏
Do you anticipate possible questions and objections?	❏	❏	❏
When communicating, do you get to the point as quickly as possible?	❏	❏	❏
Do you communicate clearly?	❏	❏	❏
Do you use language that is understood and accepted?	❏	❏	❏
Do you communicate in a relevant and logical order?	❏	❏	❏
Do you avoid repeating yourself?	❏	❏	❏
After the communication, do you encourage feedback?	❏	❏	❏
Do you respond favourably to questions and objections?	❏	❏	❏
Do you see them as an opportunity to clarify, correct or reinforce your message?	❏	❏	❏
Do you remain polite and courteous?	❏	❏	❏
Do you view communication as a two-way process?	❏	❏	❏
Is it important that you communicate with your team?	❏	❏	❏

themselves – plays a significant role in the development of a winning team. An ongoing, two-way exchange of information and feedback helps to scotch gossip, reduce confusion, settle problems more quickly and improve relationships in general. It is essential that everybody talks to one another regularly both at formal meetings and informally as work is being done, to put forward and agree upon instructions, advice and suggestions and to hear and deal with opinions, comments and worries. The questionnaire on page 19 may enable you to decide if you and your team are communicating well, and should provide some pointers for improvements, as and where appropriate.

Further reading

BELBIN R. M. *Team Roles at Work*. Oxford, Butterworth-Heinemann, 1993.

CHAUDHRY-LAWTON R., LAWTON R., MURPHY K. and TERRY A *Quality: Change through teamwork*. London, Random House, 1994.

HARDINGHAM J. and ROYAL J. *Pulling Together: Teamwork in practice*. London, Institute of Personnel and Development, 1994.

MARCHINGTON M. *Managing the Team*. Oxford, Blackwell, 1992.

WILSON G. *Self-managing Work Teams*. London, Financial Times/Pitman Publishing, 1994.

4

 **Improving Jobs**

If staff are motivated by the people around them, then it is logical that they will be affected at least equally by the work they are doing within their organisation. You may be in a position to improve their jobs, perhaps substantially in some instances. If so, you should appreciate the importance of job enjoyment, appraise employees and their employment and subsequently set about rearranging their workload, as appropriate.

Appreciating job enjoyment

Each and every individual – no matter who they are – wishes to enjoy the work that they do. What they need and want from their specific job will vary from one person to another, but three main areas will usually be of common concern:

- content
- security
- prospects.

Content

A 'job' might be said to be 'a collection of tasks and duties', and an employee's enjoyment will thus depend largely upon whether or not he or she is happy with the particular mix allocated to his or her position. Clearly, everyone is different with regard to what they want, although they will probably all view tasks and duties in the same way – in terms of their degree of difficulty, variety and responsibility. Some people will wish to do easy, routine tasks with little or no responsibility attached. Others prefer harder and challenging, ever-changing activities, with plenty of responsibilities . The majority of the workforce may well be somewhere between these two extremes.

Security

Most employees who work on a part- or full-time basis will wish to feel confident that their employment is secure both now *and* for the foreseeable future. It will be hard – if not virtually impossible – to motivate someone who believes that his or her job could end at any time. Not surprisingly, the person will be more concerned about finding a replacement position as quickly as possible rather than putting any (soon to be wasted) energy and effort into the present one. People's workrate and performance can be expected to be high *only if* they feel they are here to stay, and will share in the consequences of their hard work and successes.

Prospects

Those members of staff who wish to turn up, do a simple job without responsibilities and go home will be relatively happy if they believe that this work is secure. Nonetheless, any employee who wants to acquire more difficult, varied and responsible tasks and duties will not feel satisfied for long. They will be motivated to keep working hard and well *only if* there are clear and distinct opportunities for transfers and promotions to even more challenging, better jobs. If these prospects do not exist and employees feel they have gone as far as they can within the firm, then they are likely to be demotivated and to look to have their wants and needs fulfilled elsewhere, in another organisation.

Appraising employees and employment

Conscious of the significance of job enjoyment, you would be wise to see if all the people working with you are well matched to their employment. If not, you should try to do something about it. One after the other, you should contemplate:

- the employee
- the job
- the organisation.

The employee

Looking in turn at each of the employees working with you, it is imperative that you discover what they personally want from the job, with particular regard to its content, security and prospects. Talk to them individually when the opportunity arises, asking them about their work; what they like or dislike about it; enjoy or detest doing; their hopes and fears, concerns and worries; what they feel would improve their job; where they want to be next year, in five years' time, or whenever. Always ask – *never* assume that you know the answers yourself.

The job

The next step is to study the job in some detail to decide how far it meets the employee's wants and needs. Consider its title, location and purpose, whom the employee answers to, is in charge of and deals with on a regular or occasional basis. Contemplate the main tasks and responsibilities, how they should be completed, and the various standards and goals that must be maintained and achieved, as appropriate. Think about the skills, knowledge and expertise needed to do the job well. Build up this understanding by watching the work being done, and even doing it yourself. Check business records such as job descriptions and appraisal forms. Chat informally to colleagues, especially those in similar jobs. Know that job inside out, as if it were your own – and decide if it and the employee are well matched.

The organisation

It is essential that each job is put into context both in relation to other jobs and to the firm itself. View your existing team and the wider workforce in terms of their workload, skills, abilities and ages, trying to calculate when and to where some people may be transferred or promoted, or who could be made redundant or retired, and so forth. You may have access to the firm's current organisation chart, or even to its overall personnel plan – if so, these should be read carefully to gain a fuller picture of the possible security and prospects for each employee.

You also need to find out all you can about your organisation's plans – perhaps it is moving into new product or geographical markets – and their potential effect on your team and the workforce in general. Similarly, you must discover everything about developments in the market-place and contemplate the probable impact on your firm. Whether by checking memos, reading in-house reports, attending meetings, studying trade findings or whatever, you should stay up to date. Obviously, you may not be able to have a big influence (if any) on your colleagues' security and prospects, but at least you will be aware of the overall situation and can perhaps manoeuvre employees into the right positions accordingly.

Rearranging the workload

Ideally, all of your colleagues will be suited to their workload, and motivated by it. However, it is likely that in reality some will not be well matched, and may be dissatisfied and demotivated as a consequence. You will need to do what you can to remedy such a situation, typically by:

- rotating jobs
- enlarging jobs
- enriching jobs
- combining techniques.

Rotating jobs

Job rotation involves teaching staff to do various jobs and then switching them regularly from one to another, either upon request or at set intervals. As an example, shop employees are shown how to work in the storeroom, on the salesfloor and in the office, consequently taking it in turns to adopt these roles. A major benefit of rotation is that it may help to relieve the boredom and frustration of doing the same work over and over again. The main drawback is that people might not do any job long enough to reach and maintain acceptable standards of workrate and performance. They do many jobs inadequately, rather than one well!

Enlarging jobs

Enlargement is a technique whereby jobs are expanded to include the tasks and duties in the stage immediately before and/or after an employee's role in a production or distribution process. For example, a production-line worker who has previously completed one or two stages of a particular sequence now attends to all of them, thus personally completing a finished product. In its favour, this can make a job less specialised and monotonous, allowing employees to complete more varied tasks, but without necessarily increasing the degree of difficulty involved or letting employees actually master any of the tasks particularly well.

Enriching jobs

Jobs are 'enriched' by giving staff more complex and difficult tasks to do, and adding on responsibilities – potentially, this provides employees with all of the challenges, variety and responsibility that they can handle. As an example, a personal assistant takes over some of his or her boss's workload, making key decisions on occasion. The advantages may be that people are stretched, use untapped skills and abilities and, hopefully, become more capable and happier than before. The disadvantages may be that staff might not want or be up to the work and – just as significantly – others around them may feel resentful if *their* workload remains the same, or feel threatened that they might even lose their employment as a result of these changes.

Combining techniques

Typically, you will blend these various job improvement techniques together. Whatever you do, your aim should be to enable each person to use as many of his or her skills as they want to, providing work that is neither so simple that people feel it is beneath them nor so difficult that they struggle and become dispirited. Redesigned jobs should offer variety too, allowing staff to believe they are making a worthwhile contribution to the firm. They ought to give employees some authority as well, to take control and make decisions, however limited that may be. People should also have the opportunity to work with others: no matter what the job, nearly everyone wants some form of regular contact with their colleagues.

It is wise to examine the three approaches to decide which one (or combination) is most suitable in any specific situation. Job rotation and enlargement may offer some variety, but might not necessarily make the person feel he or she is making a more meaningful contribution to the business: after all, the alternative or extra activities often tend to be rather similar in many respects. Job enrichment can provide an employee with the chance to take control and make decisions – if this is what is wanted – but can cause ill-feeling amongst his or her colleagues.

Regardless of your decision, you should consult people before making any adjustments, however minor those may be. To implement changes without considering feelings and opinions can generate enormous and counter-productive resentment. So talk to those employees whose jobs might be affected *and* their fellow workers. Hear what they have to say and take notice of their comments and suggestions. Listen to their ideas for improvement, even if they seem impractical. Work through your plans and ideas, agreeing on amendments to be made, and when they should be brought in. Make changes slowly and methodically, giving everyone the opportunity to adjust to them. Monitor these changes, evaluating them with the workforce and implementing further amendments, if necessary. As always, work *together* – as a team.

Further reading

MITCHELL STEWART A. *Empowering People*. London, Institute of Management/Pitman Publishing, 1994.

TYLCZAK L. *Effective Employee Participation*. London, Kogan Page, 1990.

5

Developing People

Staff development might be described as 'the systematic and continual process of improving employees so that they make the fullest possible use of their abilities', thus benefiting both them *and* the firm. If people are to be motivated in this way, then you have to approach the whole process in a clear and logical manner, typically by encouraging self-development, training staff where appropriate and last – but definitely not least – by assessing employees to see that they are achieving as much as they can.

Encouraging self-development

If staff are to be *and* feel fully developed, then it is sensible to help them to set their own limits and targets to work within and towards so that they will be motivated and satisfied when they achieve what they set out to do. You need to encourage people around you to:

- define development areas
- write a personal assessment
- compose an action plan.

Define development areas

Most employees will be conscious of those areas of their performance that need to be developed, perhaps substantially in some instances. Three main areas have been identified here – remedial, developmental and creative. Remedial action will need to be implemented if a person has to improve certain aspects of his or her performance that are simply not up to standard. Developmental activities will have to take place if he or she has to gain additional skills, knowledge and expertise to cope with future work, possibly resulting from a transfer or promotion. Creative activities must be used if the employee needs to learn better ways of handling existing work and/or ways of dealing with new tasks or duties.

Write a personal assessment

Aware of the probable areas for development, members of your team should move on to assess themselves. Getting them to do this in writing is often a good way of focusing their attention completely on the task in hand. You may wish to provide them with a check-list of questions such as the one laid out overleaf, which will help them to think about their job, personality, knowledge, skills and relationships in the workplace. From their answers, they should be able to piece together a SWOT analysis like the one shown as Figure 5.1, which highlights their individual strengths and weaknesses as well as the opportunities for, and threats against, improving their overall performance.

Compose an action plan

Referring to the areas for development and personal assessment, employees should be ready to compose an action plan, incorporating what has to be done to enable them to improve and maintain their targets in the short, medium and long term. Let them decide what help is needed, which will typically include further job rotation, enlargement and enrichment, and some form of training. Get them to provide targets that *they* wish to achieve – as always, they will be spurred on more by these than by ones imposed on them by you or the firm, even though the targets will (hopefully) be similar, if not the same. An example of an action plan format is given in Figure 5.2.

Training staff

Training plays a major role in developing people successfully. Most members of staff like to be trained: they see it as a break in their routine, an opportunity to learn something new and a perk, perhaps even a reward for doing well. As important, training gives employees the skills, knowledge and expertise to do their jobs competently; keeps them up to date with changes and developments; and ensures they are ready and able to be transferred and promoted in due course. To train your team, you have to:

- spot requirements
- choose a method
- devise a programme
- evaluate the programme.

CHECK-LIST: SELF-ASSESSMENT QUESTIONS

Answering these questions will help people to gain a fuller and better understanding of their job, personality, knowledge, skills and relationships with those around them.

What exactly does your job involve?

What is its key purpose?

What are the main tasks and duties?

Are these all being completed properly and on time?

What are the major responsibilities?

Are these being handled well?

What standards must be reached?

Are they being reached and maintained?

What targets must be achieved?

Are they being achieved?

What are your personal, departmental and organisational goals?

Are these being fulfilled?

How would you describe your personality?

What are your strengths as a person?

How can they be built upon?

What are your weaknesses?

How can these be improved?

How well do you know your job, and all aspects of it?

How might you increase your knowledge, or gain it faster?

How well do you know the job that you might be transferred or promoted to?

How might you obtain an improved understanding of it?

What skills do you possess?

How well do you carry out the various aspects of your job?

What additional skills will you need to acquire for your next job?

How do you think you could gain these extra skills?

How do you get on with your colleagues?

How well do you get along with your line manager?

How well do you mix with other people?

How could you improve your relationships?

Figure 5.1

'SWOT' ANALYSIS

	STRENGTHS	WEAKNESSES	OPPORTUNITIES	THREATS
JOB				
PERSONALITY				
KNOWLEDGE				
SKILLS				
RELATIONSHIPS				

Figure 5.2

ACTION PLAN FORMAT

	TARGETS	HELP REQUIRED	ACHIEVED BY	MONITORED BY
SHORT TERM				
MEDIUM TERM				
LONG TERM				

Spot requirements

Training needs have first to be identified. This can be done in various ways, most notably through informal chats and meetings with individuals and through discussions with the whole team. Possibly, a person may approach you with a question that suggests a basic lack of knowledge which has to be remedied. Alternatively, the team may express concern about implementing a new safety procedure, a revised work practice, or whatever. Other ways of recognising needs include studying expected staff changes, the firm's plans and external developments in the market-place. For example, knowing that someone is about to leave and has to be replaced, revamped goods are to be made, and/or new technology is to be introduced will all indicate training is required.

Choose a method

There are three main training methods: 'on the job' training, 'off the job' training, and 'distance learning'. 'On the job' training usually involves an employee watching an experienced colleague performing an activity, and then tackling it under supervision. This trainer-trainee relationship continues on a 'watching and doing' basis until the activity has been mastered. In its favour, this method satisfies needs easily, because the trainer can go faster or slower as required; the trainee gains hands-on experience; and it is relatively inexpensive, although the cost of taking the trainer away from other work has to be considered. Against it, there may be insufficient in-house skills to train people properly. Equipment and facilities may be substandard too. Even if potentially good trainers exist, they may resent having to do the job!

'Off the job' training is a method whereby staff are trained by specialists, either on the firm's property or elsewhere, at a local college or nearby hotel. Here, courses are run by highly experienced experts; up-to-date information, equipment and facilities are provided; and fresh, often innovative, ideas and opinions are put across to the employees. However, these courses may not match people's exact requirements. Typically, they will be taught too much business theory, which is sometimes difficult to relate to work practices. Also, they tend to be expensive, especially when fees are added together with travel expenses, lunch allowances *and* lost production.

'Distance learning' is another popular method, with employees learning about new topics through correspondence courses supported by books, audio and video tapes, and tutors available by telephone and/or post. Clearly, there are advantages to this approach: training materials are presented professionally, new information and viewpoints can be put across and, not least, people can study when and where they want *and* work at their own speed. However, disadvantages exist too: courses are relatively expensive and may comprise more theory than practice; employees need to be highly self-motivated to work hard in their own time; and they cannot benefit from the immediate feedback of an on-the-spot trainer.

Devise a programme

It is not easy to decide which training method to use, because there are numerous, influential factors. You should think about *what* needs to be taught: a soon-to-be promoted employee who has to find out what the new job involves might be trained by the present incumbent, whilst staff who have to learn about new technology may gain more from off-the-job training. Contemplate *who* is best qualified to train your people: you may believe you are ideal, but lack the time to do it properly. Keen and experienced colleagues or external specialists may be a more sensible choice.

Consider *where* staff should be trained. For example, your firm may have the equipment and facilities, but on-the-job training may disrupt and annoy other employees. Think *how long* training is likely to take in this instance. If it is going to be a lengthy process, it may be wise to arrange for it to be carried out in the person's own time, through distance learning. Take account of *how much* the various training methods will cost as well – in both financial terms, such as fees and transport, and with regard to the time involved for everyone concerned.

Evaluate the programme

Each and every training programme must be evaluated carefully to see that employees have been given the necessary skills, knowledge and expertise, are ready for promotion, or whatever. You should talk to the trainees to find out what their views are; whether they enjoyed it; whether it was useful, too easy or hard; how it could be improved; and what other training is still required. Of course, it is essential that you seek their opinions not only to learn about the course but also to show interest in them and respect for their feelings. Nevertheless, be slightly sceptical of what they say – they may praise it because it was enjoyable and although this is important, it must have been useful too.

Talk to the trainer as well, to hear what he or she has to say, and to find out whether the trainees have obtained fresh information, acquired new skills and made progress. Again, be slightly cynical: those trainers involved with off-the-job training or distance learning may be reluctant to criticise a trainee, because it could imply there are shortcomings with the courses. Watch the trainees at work yourself to discover if they have mastered additional activities and whether their workrate and performance have improved accordingly. This is the 'acid test'!

Assessing employees

Often overlooked as part of the development process, staff assessment – or 'appraisal' – serves several purposes. It enables you to monitor progress, identify and praise strengths, and recognise weaknesses, consequently working together with the employee to remedy them. Amongst its other benefits, it gives you the chance to spot prospective candidates for transfer and promotion at the earliest opportunity. Knowing that they are being appraised – informally on an ongoing basis and more formally on an annual one – will keep employees working hard and well. With regard to the annual assessment, you need to know what to do:

- before the interview
- during the interview
- after the interview.

Before the interview

Before the interview you should draw up a check-list of points you wish to discuss – perhaps attendance, timekeeping, personal appearance, general conduct, work performance, work relations, strengths, weaknesses and recommendations for the future. You may wish to put these into a clear and simple appraisal form (see Figure 5.3). Involve your colleague by talking about the interview at least one week in advance, so he or she has time to think everything through, and prepare comments and suggestions. Stress this is an informal and relaxed meeting: you are working *together* to maintain and improve upon developments to date! If you have composed a form, hand this over to indicate the areas to be dealt with in turn.

Prepare for the interview by reading through your check-list or form, thinking about the employee's recent workrate, performance and general development, and calculating the topics you are going to cover and in which order – usually the same sequence as the form. Decide where to hold the interview – preferably somewhere quiet where you can both concentrate without interruptions from the telephone or colleagues, or noise from adjacent rooms. Make sure there are no distractions in the interview room itself such as bright sunlight, a cluttered desk or an uncomfortable chair: you do need to have your team member at his or her ease.

Figure 5.3

ASSESSMENT FORM

NAME:	
JOB TITLE:	
LENGTH OF EMPLOYMENT:	
DATE OF ASSESSMENT:	

Please state whether the employee is [A] excellent [B] very good [C] satisfactory [D] unsatisfactory in each of the following categories. Provide additional comments where appropriate.

ATTENDANCE

TIMEKEEPING

PERSONAL APPEARANCE

GENERAL CONDUCT

WORK PERFORMANCE	

WORK RELATIONS	

Please summarise your assessment of the employee and provide any recommendations that may help to improve his or her overall performance.

STRENGTHS

WEAKNESSES

RECOMMENDATIONS

ASSESSED BY:	**AGREED BY:**
NAME:	**NAME:**
JOB TITLE:	**JOB TITLE:**
SIGNATURE:	**SIGNATURE:**

During the interview

Try not to keep the interviewee waiting: it seems rude and uncaring, and increases tension which is not conducive to the relaxed and co-operative atmosphere you are seeking to establish. Greet him or her with a warm smile and handshake, making polite conversation as you walk to the quiet room. Show the interviewee to a seat, and explain the purpose of the interview again. Keep everything very low key and informal. Work together through the appraisal check-list or form, one topic at a time. Ask him or her for a self-assessment of each different area. Pick up and agree upon his or her strengths, praising them fully. Encouragement is a great motivator. Comment on weaknesses too, but without being destructive: they are going to be remedied, perhaps through more development and training!

Hear what the interviewer has to say: be seen to listen to his or her ideas, suggestions *and* any problems or concerns which may be affecting workrate and performance. Perhaps he or she is worried about health and safety, pay or other potential demotivators. These issues need to be addressed. Conclude the interview by completing the assessment form together. This can then be held on file so that subsequent progress and development can be checked next time around. Summarise the main points again, praising successes and agreeing how shortcomings can be remedied, or at least much reduced. Decide when you will meet once more to reassess the situation. End with another warm smile and handshake, thanking the interviewee for his or her time. Always close on a positive, upbeat note.

After the interview

It is essential that you follow through on the appraisal interview: after all, staff development needs to be a systematic and continual process if it is to be successful. Carry out any agreed measures to reduce or eliminate identified weaknesses, typically arranging for extra on-the-job training to take place, or to register the employee on a respected, off-the-job training course. Keep a close watch on the person's progress, encouraging him or her at each and every opportunity. Then meet again at the agreed time to conduct the next staff assessment interview – and to praise and congratulate him or her on his or her successes. Hopefully the employee will have developed as far as possible by this time – and will feel fully satisfied as a consequence!

Further reading

DENT F., MACGREGOR B. and WILLS S. *A Guide to Self-Managed Development*. London, Ashridge/Financial Times/Pitman Publishing, 1994.

HARRISON R. *Employee Development*. London, Institute of Personnel Management, 1992.

TAYLOR D. and BISHOP S. *Readymade Activities for Developing Your Staff*. London, Institute of Management/Pitman Publishing, 1994.

TRUELOVE S. (ed.) *Handbook of Training and Development*. Oxford, Blackwell, 1994.

6

Paying Staff

Pay and related financial benefits have a part to play in motivating people, although money is more likely to be a potential demotivator than a powerful motivator. Even though you may not have much influence here, you should develop a fuller understanding of pay and its possible effects on motivation by considering pay levels, thinking about pay systems and contemplating the overall pay package, including fringe benefits provided by your firm.

Considering pay levels

Clearly, the basic level of pay received is important to staff – too low and they will probably do no more than the bare minimum and may even leave as soon as possible, about right (whatever that might be) and they will feel satisfied, leaving you in a position to motivate them through various pay schemes or in other ways, such as by being a good leader, working as a team, and so on. The 'right' level in your situation can perhaps be worked out by looking at numerous factors:

- employees' value
- colleagues' pay
- other benefits
- your firm
- the market-place
- the law.

Employees' value

All staff want to feel that they are earning a fair and reasonable amount of money – in essence, that they are getting what they deserve. Every employee will have some sense of what they are worth, basing this (perhaps subconsciously) on their perceived skills, knowledge and experience, relating these to the workload, and then building up an idea of what they should be paid. If on less than that, they will inevitably feel disgruntled.

Colleagues' pay

Similarly, people need to feel that they are being paid sums in proportion to those given to fellow-workers in their department, and nearby ones too. Often, they will compare their own capabilities, expertise and workload with those of their immediate colleagues, and others with whom they come into contact on a regular or occasional basis. Again, they will develop some idea of what everyone is worth and should be paid – and will resent certain employees and the firm itself if their and others' pay is not what they feel it ought to be.

Other benefits

Fringe benefits such as discounts on goods and services, travel allowances, company cars, sickness and healthcare schemes and the like combine with pay to form an overall package for employees. As with pay itself, people will inevitably make judgements about what they and others are being given, and will be dissatisfied if they are not getting what they think they deserve or if they feel colleagues are obtaining benefits that they have not earned through hard work and achievement.

Your firm

The size and success of the organisation you work for will have an impact on what staff believe they ought to receive in terms of basic pay (and indeed, fringe benefits). A business that is small and perhaps struggling to survive cannot be expected to pay out generous wages, and most employees will recognise and accept this. However, a business that is either growing or is already large and successful may well be expected to share its success with its workforce, typically by paying higher wages than its smaller competitors.

The market-place

The majority of staff will be conscious of what is happening outside the firm, and this will influence their views on their pay. In particular, they may be aware of the general employment situation. If this is characterised by high unemployment, they might feel grateful to be working at all. If, however, there are plenty of job opportunities, they might start to feel dissatisfied with their position. They will also tend to compare their wages with what could be earned in a similar job elsewhere, and want to know if they are doing better with your firm, or worse. Inflation is often significant too, with annual pay increases expected in order to keep pace with rising prices.

The law

It is important that the law is complied with, not only because of the possible legal consequences of a breach but also because of its effects on motivation. Individual pay deals – including entitlement to fringe benefits – made on recruitment must be honoured. To adhere to the Equal Pay Act 1970, people doing the same or broadly similar jobs *or* work of equal value (in that a comparable degree of skill, expertise and effort is required) need to be given equal pay, regardless of their sex, job, or number of hours worked. The only exception is when more money is paid after a certain number of years of service. Wage agreements reached during negotiations with staff representatives have to be fulfilled as well.

Thinking about pay systems

There are many different types of pay scheme, and often more than one will operate within the same firm. It is sensible to be aware of the most popular systems and their pros and cons, particularly with regard to motivating people. If you are in a position to influence or change the payment scheme (or schemes) used in your organisation, you can then make a choice about which is the right one (or ones) in your circumstances. Thus, you need to consider:

- payment by function
- payment by attendance
- payment by results
- making the choice.

Payment by function

This is a system whereby staff are paid a set salary for doing a specific job, regardless of the hours worked, or their work-rate or performance. Typically, they will be given a fixed annual sum, paid monthly in equal instalments, in arrears. In its favour, such a scheme is simple to administer, and the total wages bill can be anticipated in advance, which aids forecasting and budgeting. However, it does mean that employees are being paid even when they are not working hard or well – or at all! There is no incentive to do more than the minimum needed to retain employment. Therefore, you may have to monitor employees closely, continually encouraging them, which can be both stressful and time-consuming.

Payment by attendance

Here, people are paid according to the number of hours or days actually worked, with wages being handed over on a daily, weekly or monthly basis, as relevant. Clearly, this scheme is easy to operate and it is straightforward enough to calculate the wages due both now and in the future. Also, staff do physically need to work in order to be paid, so there is an inbuilt 'value for money' element in the system. Nevertheless, it cannot really motivate employees to do more, or to improve. Lazy ones will try to hide behind more industrious colleagues, doing as little as possible. Again, they will need to be watched carefully, and chivvied along, which is a tricky skill to acquire, and use well.

Payment by results

With this scheme – and there are numerous individual, group and company-wide variations of it – staff receive a basic wage according to function and/or hours worked, with additional sums being linked to results – the number of goods produced, sold and so forth. The main benefit of this type of system is that it should inspire employees to work harder, so that their pay-packets are larger. Group and company schemes can also improve teamwork and morale. Nevertheless, there are drawbacks: it can be hard and time-consuming to devise a good *and* viable system; it may be difficult to calculate money due, which hinders budgeting as well; and quality of work is often sacrificed for quantity.

Making the choice

Evidently, the 'ideal' payment scheme does not exist: each system has its own strengths *and* weaknesses. However, the best scheme in the circumstances is probably one that suits the firm, its activities *and* the workforce – no easy task! Perhaps the business does not want continually to supervise hourly-paid staff, and wishes to build a self-motivating element into its pay. Quantity of output may be more relevant than quality – or vice versa. Employees may want stable, level pay or might prefer lower basic wages, with the potential to earn bonuses. It is difficult to devise a system that suits all, and often a compromise needs to be reached that keeps everyone reasonably contented.

Whatever the system – and it will usually be a mix of basic payments with bonuses – it must be easy for the firm to measure, check and pay, *and* be affordable too. Staff need to understand exactly what they have to do to succeed, and all employees have to be given an equal chance to earn more. Ideally, bonus pay should be linked to workrate *and* performance, and must be handed over often and on time if it is to continue to motivate – too long a wait, and workers will lose interest. There should not be too much emphasis on bonuses – 80 per cent basic, 20 per cent bonus is about right – as quality will otherwise become less important than quantity, and an overcompetitive environment may develop as well.

Contemplating the pay package

Of course, there is more to 'pay' than just the money received at the end of the week, the following month or whenever. Numerous other benefits could be said to comprise the overall pay package. The following ones may not motivate people, but can help to make them feel good, and receptive to being motivated in some other way:

- discounts
- financial assistance
- paid time-off
- sick-pay schemes
- health insurance schemes
- pension schemes.

Discounts

Many organisations now offer a mixture of discounts and subsidies to their employees – perhaps 10 per cent or more off their products and services, low-priced drinks and snacks from vending machines, in-house cafeteria facilities, luncheon vouchers for local restaurants, cut-price admission to nearby leisure complexes, and so on. To be worthwhile, such benefits need to be valued by staff. For example, there is little point in offering discounts on industrial components, because employees are unlikely to want them. Also – and it is an obvious fact which is often overlooked – the firm must be able to afford them. Clearly, whereas a small concern may have the money to install a vending machine, it will not be able to afford a cafeteria, which is expensive to set up and run.

Financial assistance

It is common practice for some firms to help their workforce financially, both in an informal and a more formal capacity – advances on wages now and then, an allowance for motor and petrol costs or even a company car, (part-) payment towards a railway season ticket, a low-cost or interest-free loan, and so forth. Again, such assistance should be matched to the needs of employees and must be affordable: the business should not endanger its cash flow or viability just to satisfy its staff. Any advances, loans and the like ought to be noted down in writing, or be subject to a legally binding agreement, if more appropriate.

Paid time-off

Often, holidays and time-off are of greater concern to some people than discounts, subsidies and other financial perks. Holiday entitlements, ranging from about 18 days plus public and bank holidays for juniors to 30 or more for longer-serving senior staff, are a potential source of grievance and cause for demotivation. Everyone wishes to feel they are receiving a satisfactory amount, relative to their age, experience, status and colleagues. Also, they want to go away when they want, subject to the reasonable needs of the firm. A fair system for choosing holiday dates must operate. Typically, those at the top pick their first week's holiday and so on down through the organisation. They then select their second week, mindful of who else will be away at certain times and the minimum staffing levels which need to be maintained.

Reasonable, paid time-off is a legal right in many instances, and must be given readily if staff are not to become angry and dissatisfied. Hopefully, such leave will be taken at mutually convenient times wherever possible. Pregnant women are entitled to paid time-off for antenatal care appointments made on the advice of a doctor, midwife or health visitor. They must have made an appointment, asked for time-off and be able to show, on request, proof of pregnancy and an appointment card – but it may seem churlish to ask for these. Employees under notice of redundancy are allowed paid time-off to look for work or to arrange retraining. Strictly speaking, they should have been employed for 16 hours plus per week for two years, or for between eight and 16 hours per week for five years, to be given this – but to retain everyone's goodwill it may be wise to be flexible.

Union safety officers have a legal entitlement to paid time-off to receive appropriate training – and this can benefit the business too, because they will be able to offer advice on maintaining a safe and healthy workplace. Other union officials are allowed paid time-off to conduct their duties during working hours *if* the firm agrees to this. Obviously, it will do little for morale and employer/employee relations if reasonable requests are refused. Staff who carry out public duties (perhaps as local councillors) or who are called for jury service are normally entitled to time-off, although this need not be paid. Time-off may also be requested for paternity leave or bereavement, and the amount given in these circumstances, and whether it is paid at all, is at the firm's discretion. It may be sensible to err on the generous side to sustain a happy, satisfied team.

Sick-pay schemes

Although most workers are eligible for Statutory Sick Pay (SSP), this is paid at a low rate in comparison with their usual salary, which is distressing for those who are actually off sick and a constant worry for others who may go off sick in the future. Thus, many businesses set up their own sick-pay scheme, often related to length of service. For example, an employee with one year's service may be given full pay for the first four weeks of sickness, followed by half-pay for the next four, and basic SSP thereafter. Clearly, such a scheme can be costly – although it can be largely offset by taking out appropriate insurance beforehand – but it does help to develop a more contented workforce.

Health insurance schemes

Some businesses arrange private health insurance for key – or all – members of their staff through organisations such as BUPA. Many people feel safer and more secure if they know that quick and efficient treatment is available for them if they fall ill. However, a number may feel that private health care is immoral, and their views will need to be both taken into account and treated respectfully if they are not to become upset and aggrieved with the firm. Swift medical care for sick employees is beneficial to the business as well, because they will be able to return to work that much sooner than they would otherwise do.

Pension schemes

Most people worry about their future from time to time. Older employees in particular will probably be concerned about their retirement and its financial consequences – whether they can afford to live on the state pension, whether sufficient additional provision has been made by them, and the like. Those firms that arrange for their (older) staff to receive guidance on retirement planning and personal pension schemes, or even establish a company scheme into which contributions can be paid on a regular, long-term basis will go some way towards easing fears and developing a happy and satisfied workforce.

Further reading

BOWEY A. *Managing Salary and Wage Systems*. Aldershot, Gower, 1994.

CANNELL M. and WOOD S. *Incentive Pay: Impact and evolution*. London, Institute of Personnel Management, 1992.

FRIEDMAN B. *The Stoy Hayward Guide to Effective Staff Incentives*. London, Kogan Page, 1990.

HUME D. *Reward Management*. Oxford, Blackwell, 1995.

7

Providing a Safe and Healthy Workplace

The workplace is widely considered to play a role in staff motivation, albeit as more of a potential demotivating than a motivating influence. It needs to be satisfactory for employees to be motivated in some way, such as through leadership and teamwork. If it is unsatisfactory, they will be distracted by it, and less inclined to work hard and well. So far as possible, you need to try to ensure safe working conditions and to build a healthy environment. Also, you should know something about health and safety law, and your firm's responsibilities in this field.

Ensuring safe working conditions

Your organisation is legally obliged to provide a workplace in which you and your colleagues can work safely, without (or with minimal) risk of injuries or illnesses resulting from it. Clearly, people cannot work – let alone be motivated to work efficiently and effectively – if they are constantly worrying about slippery floors, unprotected machinery, unsafe work practices, general security and the like. Opposite is a questionnaire which may enable you to decide whether you are working in truly safe conditions. If not, you will want to discuss the matter with your line manager, or a health and safety specialist within the firm.

Building a healthy environment

Of course, it is important that premises not only achieve minimal safety standards but are positively healthy too. Employees who are working in a pleasant atmosphere are much more likely to be receptive to being motivated than those labouring in a workplace that is cramped, too hot or cold, noisy and so on. The questionnaire on page 48 could help you to judge whether you work in a healthy environment. If not, improvements can often be made by carrying out various minor tasks. Alternatively, shortcomings will need to be referred to those higher up in the organisation.

ARE YOU WORKING IN SAFE CONDITIONS?

Can you say 'yes' to all of these questions? If not, you are probably working in unsafe conditions, and improvements need to be made – fast!

	Yes	Sometimes	No
Are floors, passages and stairs solid, clean and free from obstacles?	❏	❏	❏
Are floor openings covered or guarded?	❏	❏	❏
Are steps, corners and obstacles marked clearly?	❏	❏	❏
Are fire escapes unlocked and unobstructed?	❏	❏	❏
Are plant, equipment and machinery fenced off, if appropriate?	❏	❏	❏
Are they in good, working order?	❏	❏	❏
Do clear guidelines exist for operating equipment and machinery?	❏	❏	❏
Are these guidelines updated regularly?	❏	❏	❏
Are operatives trained and retrained, when necessary?	❏	❏	❏
Are protective clothing and equipment provided for users?	❏	❏	❏
Are these worn and used properly?	❏	❏	❏
Are safe work practices adhered to?	❏	❏	❏
Are equipment and machinery checked regularly?	❏	❏	❏
Are they repaired or replaced, as required?	❏	❏	❏
Is a trained first aider on the premises?	❏	❏	❏
Does everyone know what to do in an accident or emergency situation?	❏	❏	❏
Are accident and emergency procedures tested regularly?	❏	❏	❏
Is a fully stocked, first aid box kept on the property?	❏	❏	❏
Does everyone know where it is, and how to use it?	❏	❏	❏
Do procedures exist to protect staff against customers?	❏	❏	❏
Are these tested regularly?	❏	❏	❏
Are employees protected against vandals and burglars by locks, bolts and alarms?	❏	❏	❏
Are these visual deterrents checked regularly?	❏	❏	❏

ARE YOU WORKING IN A HEALTHY ENVIRONMENT?

If you can answer 'yes' to the following questions, you may be working in a healthy environment. If you cannot, then you should be seeking to improve your workplace as quickly as possible.

	Yes	Sometimes	No
Is this a spacious workplace?	❏	❏	❏
Does everyone have their own personal space?	❏	❏	❏
Do they have somewhere to put their personal possessions?	❏	❏	❏
Are seats and benches comfortable?	❏	❏	❏
Can equipment and machinery be operated easily?	❏	❏	❏
Can everybody move around comfortably?	❏	❏	❏
Is the temperature acceptable everywhere?	❏	❏	❏
Is suitable work clothing provided, if appropriate?	❏	❏	❏
Are all areas well ventilated?	❏	❏	❏
Is there a 'no smoking' policy?	❏	❏	❏
Is heating and ventilation equipment in good working order?	❏	❏	❏
Is it serviced and repaired regularly?	❏	❏	❏
Are the premises well lit?	❏	❏	❏
Is there extra, local lighting, where necessary?	❏	❏	❏
Is sufficient emergency lighting available, if needed?	❏	❏	❏
Are outside areas lit at night?	❏	❏	❏
Are lights and windows clean?	❏	❏	❏
Are equipment, machinery and processes quiet?	❏	❏	❏
Are noisy equipment, machinery and processes identified with warning signs?	❏	❏	❏
Is there a pleasant, well-equipped room or area for drinking?	❏	❏	❏
Are hanging spaces and lockers provided for clothes and bags?	❏	❏	❏
Is an area set aside for drying clothes, when necessary?	❏	❏	❏
Are toilets clean, ventilated, accessible and in working order?	❏	❏	❏
Are wash basins available with hot and cold running water, soap, towels and other cleaning items?	❏	❏	❏

Knowing the law

Numerous Acts have been passed concerning health and safety in the workplace, most notably the Factories Act 1961, the Offices, Shops and Railway Premises Act 1963 and the Health and Safety Act 1974. These set out the minimum standards that must be adhered to by all firms in order to establish and maintain a healthy, safe environment. The following areas are also significant:

- risk assessments
- a policy statement
- training programmes
- registration.

Risk assessments

Your firm has a responsibility to conduct regular risk assessments of your workplace in order to check and monitor the safety of its employees. These assessments will encompass many of the questions raised in the two questionnaires in this chapter, with particular emphasis on floors, passages and stairs, plant, equipment and machinery, work systems and practices, accidents and emergencies and general security concerning safety. With regard to health, they will focus on layout and space, heating and ventilation, light and noise, plus welfare facilities. Other more specific areas will be looked at too, as relevant to your particular type and nature of business.

A policy statement

If five or more people are employed by your organisation, it has a legal duty to outline its health and safety rules and procedures in a policy document. This should be compiled after discussions with trade union safety representatives (if appropriate) and form part of the staff handbook and/or be kept on permanent display, perhaps on a noticeboard in a staff restroom. It has to be updated whenever necessary.

Training programmes

Your firm must allow trade union safety officials to take paid time-off to attend health and safety training courses. It should set up a committee to discuss health and safety issues, if requested by a union. Of equal – if not greater – relevance, staff need to be given enough information, supervision and training to maintain health and safety, day in and day out. This must be done regularly, because it is easy to forget what has been taught and to become careless and sloppy, which may lead to accidents and injuries. Also, as with risk assessments and a policy statement, it makes people feel more confident and secure about the workplace.

Registration

Shops, offices, warehouses, hotels and restaurants must register with their local authority, making themselves available for inspection and advice on health and safety matters. Other types of business, such as factories, need to be registered with the Health and Safety Executive (HSE). The address and telephone number of a regional office can be found in your local telephone directory. Like councils, the HSE will on request provide a huge amount of literature and guidance. You should encourage your firm to get in touch, if contact has not yet been established.

Further reading

BROADHURST V. A. *Health and Safety*. London, NatWest/Pitman Publishing, 1990.

SAUNDERS R. *The Safety Audit*. London, Pitman Publishing, 1993.

STRANKS J. *Health and Safety*. London, Pitman Publishing, 1994.